LEADING LIVES

Vladimir Ilyich

LENIN

DAVID DOWNING

Heinemann Library
Chicago, Illinois

Designed by AMR
Illustrated by Art Construction
Originated by Dot Gradations
Printed in China

06 05 04 03 02
10 9 8 7 6 5 4 3 2 1

Library of Congress Cataloging-in-Publication Data
Downing, David, 1946, Aug. 9
  Vladimir Ilyich Lenin / David Downing.
      p. cm. -- (Leading lives)
Summary: Follows the life of the leader of the Bolshevik Revolution, who
became the first head of the Soviet state.
  ISBN 1-58810-582-2
  1. Lenin, Vladimir Ilyich, 1870-1924--Juvenile literature. 2. Heads
of state--Soviet Union--Biography--Juvenile literature. 3.
Revolutionaries--Soviet Union--Biography--Juvenile literature. 4.
Communists--Soviet Union--Biography--Juvenile literature. 5. Soviet
Union--History--1917-1936--Juvenile literature. [1. Lenin, Vladimir
Ilyich, 1870-1924. 2. Heads of state. 3. Revolutionaries. 4. Soviet
Union--History--1917-1936.] I. Title. II. Series.
  DK254.L4 D65 2002
  947.084'1'092--dc21
                                        2001003535

Acknowledgments
The publishers would like to thank the following for permission to reproduce photographs:
Novosti, pp. 4, 6, 10, 11, 16, 17, 18, 19, 23, 28, 33, 34, 35, 38, 44, 44, 46, 48, 53; Camera Press, pp. 7, 13, 42,
45, 55; Corbis, p. 14; Popperfoto, p. 20; Hulton Archive, pp. 24, 31, 41, 51.

Cover photograph reproduced with permission of Rex Features.

Our thanks to Christopher Gibb for his comments in the preparation of this book.

Some words are shown in bold, **like this**. You can find out what they mean by looking in the glossary.

Contents

1 The Finland Station

It is late in the evening of April 3, 1917. A long train rumbles along the approach to Petrograd, the capital of Russia at the time. In one of its lighted coaches sits Vladimir Ilyich Ulyanov, better known to the world as Lenin. He is returning to Russia after ten years in exile. He has spent those years writing revolutionary books, organizing his revolutionary party, the **Bolsheviks,** and waiting for the revolution that will sweep away the Russian **Czar** and his government.

The train clanks and hisses to a halt in Petrograd's Finland Station. It is almost midnight but many are gathered to greet Lenin and the other returning exiles. There is an honor guard of revolutionary sailors on the platform, a delegation from the new Petrograd **Soviet** waiting inside the station building, and a vast crowd of sympathizers waving red banners in the square beyond.

▲ This Soviet-era painting shows Lenin speaking to the crowd outside Petrograd's Finland Station, shortly after his arrival on April 3, 1917.

Lenin steps from the train, briefly addresses the sailors, and walks through to the reception room once reserved for the czar and his family, which is now called the People's Room. The Chairman of the Petrograd Soviet steps forward to greet him, expecting a moment of shared celebration. After all, the czar and his government are gone. However, Lenin almost brushes him aside. He has not come home to celebrate what has already been achieved, but to demand more—much more.

He strides through to the main square and climbs up onto the top of an armored car that local Bolsheviks have brought along to act as a podium. He tells the hushed crowd how little the first revolution has really achieved, how little the new, temporary government will really do for ordinary people. They need another revolution, he says, a **socialist** revolution.

At this moment few agree with him. Over the next few months, however, he will win over the doubters in his own Bolshevik Party and go on to convince a majority of ordinary workers, soldiers, and other Russians that his is the right way forward. Together they will seize power, and this second revolution will turn Russia upside down. Lenin and his successors will do what has never been done before: they will try to create a government that provides absolutely everything for its citizens, who will therefore have no need for any private property.

They will fail. But the attempt, which begins in earnest here at Finland Station, will be thought by some to be the most important political event of the twentieth century. Lenin's revolution will affect everything that comes after it, both in Russia and also around the world.

Vladimir Ilyich Ulyanov, later known as Lenin, was born in the Russian town of Simbirsk on April 10, 1870. His parents Ilya and Maria already had two children—Anna and Alexander—and they would have three more after Vladimir: Olga, Dmitri, and Maria. As inspector of schools for the entire province of Simbirsk, Ilya Ulyanov held an important and respected position, and the family lived in a large house in the center of the town.

Both Ilya and Maria were well educated, and between them they instilled a love of learning in their children. The house was full of books and the family often read together in the evenings.

"Volodya"

Vladimir—or "Volodya," as the family called him—had trouble learning to walk. He was frequently falling over, banging his above-average-sized head, and roaring with frustration. He remained a noisy boy throughout his childhood, but he also began to reveal several enduring and valuable characteristics.

◀ This is the Ulyanov family in 1879. Standing, from left to right, are Olga, Alexander, and Anna. Sitting, from left to right, are Maria Alexandrovna (with Maria on her lap), Dmitri, Ilya Nikolayevich, and Vladimir Ilyich (Lenin).

People thought he was charming and likeable. Volodya found it difficult to lie, and on one occasion when he did so—denying that he had broken a vase belonging to an aunt—his mother found him crying with guilt three months later.

▲ *This is the house where Vladimir Ilyich Lenin was born in Simbirsk, which lies on the Volga River.*

Volodya was a very clever boy, and his school record, like that of his older brother Alexander, turned out to be everything his father could have wished for. Both boys attended the Simbirsk Classical Gimnazia, a school for brighter boys, from the age of nine. Both earned very good grades throughout their school careers. Volodya in particular was a very careful worker, and always paid attention to details.

A good report

"Extremely talented, consistently keen and accurate, Ulyanov in all classes was the top pupil and at the end of his course was awarded the gold medal as the most deserving pupil in performance, development, and behavior. Neither at the gimnazia [school] nor outside did any occasion come to light when Ulyanov by word or deed attracted disapproving opinion from the governing authorities or teachers . . ."

(This reference was written by Lenin's headmaster, Fyedor Kerensky. By a strange twist of fate, the government headed by Fyedor's son Alexander Kerensky was overthrown by Lenin's party in 1917.)

When he was not working, Vladimir loved to take part in outdoor activities, often in the company of his sister Olga. In the summer they could fish, swim, or go sailing on the nearby Volga River. In the long, freezing winter they could skate, ski, and go sledding.

In many ways it seems to have been a happy childhood. Vladimir was a clever, healthy boy growing up in a large, prosperous, and loving family. Indeed, some neighbors in Simbirsk even went so far as to call the Ulyanovs "the beautiful family." The children's futures seemed assured.

Russia

In the late nineteenth century, the Russian Empire included European Russia, much of Poland, the vast Asian region known as Siberia, and present-day Finland, Lithuania, Latvia, Estonia, Moldova, Belarus, Ukraine, Georgia, Azerbaijan, Armenia, Turkmenistan, Kazakstan, Uzbekistan, Kyrgyzstan, and Tajikistan. Finland and Poland became independent **states** in 1917 and 1918. The others remained part of the Union of Soviet Socialist Republics (or Soviet Union) until its breakup in the early 1990s.

Tragedies

Then, out of this clear blue sky, tragedy struck not once but twice. In 1886, when Vladimir was fifteen, Ilya Ulyanov died quite suddenly, probably from a brain hemorrhage. By this time Alexander was already at the university in the Russian capital **St. Petersburg,** and during this period of shock and grief Vladimir had to act as the man of the family. He found it difficult, and for some time his behavior was much worse than usual, but life went on. The family made efforts to economize, and Vladimir continued with his studies, expecting soon to follow his brother to the university.

▲ *This map shows the Russian Empire, around 1890.*

Ilya and Maria had always been progressive—they wanted Russia to modernize itself, to become more like the **democracies** of western Europe—but they expected change to come gradually, and to be brought about by reason and persuasion. Their eldest son Alexander, having moved from the sleepy town of Simbirsk to Russia's capital, had become very aware of how bad things really were for most of his fellow Russians. A few thousand families had most of the money and held most of the power, and millions of peasants lived as virtual slaves, many in terrible poverty. Famines were common. There was no Senate or House of Representatives, only a hereditary **czar** who ruled as he saw fit. There was no legal way of opposing this state of affairs.

9

▲ *Vladimir's brother Alexander Ulyanov is pictured here.*

There were groups of men and women who felt strongly enough about the situation to form illegal opposition groups, and by 1886 Alexander felt compelled to join one of them. This group's intention was to assassinate the **czar** in order to force a change, but the police caught them before they had time to carry out their plan. At the trial, Alexander bravely took most of the blame himself, and he was sentenced to death. On May 8, 1887, he was hanged in **St. Petersburg.**

A brother's legacy

The effect of Alexander's death on the family was devastating. Maria Ulyanova, who had still not recovered from losing her husband, was driven to thoughts of suicide. Former friends and acquaintances avoided the entire family—no one wanted to be associated with the relatives of a convicted terrorist.

Vladimir tried to comfort his mother. He sympathized with his sister Olga, who was being given the cold shoulder by classmates at school, and he played games with his younger brother and sister to take their minds off the tragedy. Vladimir kept his own feelings mostly to himself, but he might have felt angry as well as sad. He seems to have had no doubt that Alexander had acted with the best of motives. "It must mean that he had to act like this," he told a friend. "He couldn't act in any other way."

3 In His Brother's Footsteps

Despite everything, Vladimir managed to pass his final school exams with the highest grades in all ten subjects. Such grades would have warranted a place in St. Petersburg University for most young men, but not the brother of a convicted terrorist. Vladimir was forced to settle for studying law at his father's old university in Kazan, some 87 miles (140 kilometers) north of Simbirsk. The whole family decided that they would move with him.

During the summer of 1887, as he waited to start his studies, Vladimir read a great deal. One book that had belonged to Alexander appealed to him enormously.

▲ *This is Lenin in 1887, the year his brother was executed.*

The heroes of Nikolai Chernyshevski's novel *What Is to Be Done?* were **socialist** activists who were caught up in the struggle for change in the czar's Russia. Their calls for **democracy,** for **women's rights,** and for an end to the oppression of minorities all made sense to Vladimir. He may have imagined his brother, or perhaps even himself, as Chernyshevski's upright hero, righting wrongs.

Kazan

At Kazan University, Vladimir soon got involved in student politics. He was expelled for this after only three months.

Vladimir was asked to leave both the university and the city for taking part in demonstrations against the authorities. The family moved temporarily to Kokushkino, a country estate owned by his mother's family. There, Vladimir continued what he now considered his real education: reading the works of important European thinkers. He was particularly interested in the theories and political ideas of Karl Marx. When the family was allowed to return to Kazan in September 1888, Vladimir quickly renewed connections with his politically involved friends.

He wanted to resume his studies, either at Kazan University or abroad, but his requests were refused. His mother decided that they would be better off living somewhere else. A friend of Vladimir's elder sister, Anna, arranged for the purchase of a small estate further down the Volga River in the Samara region, and the family moved there in May 1889. His mother encouraged Vladimir to take part in managing the estate, but he was much more interested in continuing with school.

The reluctant lawyer

In 1890, Vladimir was allowed to resume his studies at St. Petersburg University as an **external student**—a student who studies from home. He managed to complete the four-year course in less than one, and to pass the examinations with ease. In the meantime, however, tragedy had struck the family again. After a short illness, Vladimir's favorite sister, Olga, died in **St. Petersburg** on May 8, 1891. It was the fourth anniversary of Alexander's execution. Vladimir returned to Samara and began practicing as a lawyer. He also resumed his political activity.

Karl Marx

Karl Marx was a nineteenth-century German philosopher who believed he had figured out the way that society changes. He thought that throughout history each ruling class—each group of people who dominated a society through either force, wealth, or a combination of the two—**inevitably** created its own opposition. In Marx's time the **bourgeoisie**—the owners of land, businesses, and banks—was the ruling class in the most advanced countries, but to make their world work its members needed a growing army of ordinary workers.

Marx believed that these workers would eventually get so numerous and so fed up with making money for other people that they would kick out the bourgeoisie and rule in their place. Because they would then be a large majority of the population, their rule would be fairer for most people. That type of rule would be called **socialism.**

Marx had many facts to back up his theory, and many people came to believe that he was right. These people were called **marxists** or marxist socialists.

▶ *Karl Marx was an economist, a philosopher, and the founder of modern* **communism.** *Lenin applied the ideas of Marx to Russian conditions.*

There seems to have been no doubt that Vladimir was more interested in politics than law. He was now every bit as committed to the overthrow of the **czar** and the rest of the Russian ruling class as his brother Alexander had been. The difference lay in the brothers' temperaments and the methods that they preferred. Vladimir thought his brother had been too emotional, too quick to sacrifice himself. Vladimir told himself that he would not make the same mistakes. The theories of Marx told him that time was on his side because there were wider forces working to overthrow the old order, and that the most important thing was to understand and control those forces. Vladimir believed that individual acts, no matter how brave or romantic, would achieve little or nothing.

In the summer of 1892 a famine hit the Volga region, but Vladimir, almost alone among his friends, refused to support relief efforts. The famine, he said, was a consequence of the way the country was run, and by supporting the relief efforts people were, in effect, supporting the czar. Only a revolution, he believed, could bring an end to famines.

▼ *This is the Volga River at Kazan, where Lenin attended the university in the fall of 1887.*

4 The Young Revolutionary

By the summer of 1893, Vladimir was tired of Samara and life in the provinces. He left the family home and moved to **St. Petersburg,** where he registered as an assistant to another lawyer. However, he did no legal work and relied on a monthly allowance from his mother for his living expenses. His real work was politics—reading, writing, talking, and organizing.

He had now read almost everything Marx had written, and felt able to use Marx's ideas in his own writing. His intelligence shone through at meetings, as did his leadership skills. His fellow political thinkers were not only out-argued, but were also made to question their own level of commitment. Vladimir was not prepared to give anyone an easy ride.

Although he was only 24 years old, the loss of most of his hair made him look older. There was nothing revolutionary about his appearance: he hated untidiness and waste, was careful with money, kept his beard trimmed, and his shoes well repaired. The only thing Vladimir was careless about was his own health, which was unfortunate. Most of his family seem to have suffered from stomach problems at one time or another, and his irregular eating habits took a heavy toll. He suffered badly from headaches and had trouble sleeping.

He does not seem to have been very interested in romance, but it was during this period that he met his future wife, Nadezhda Krupskaya. It is hard to know for certain, but their relationship seems to have been based on political friendship.

The future Mrs. Lenin

Nadezhda Krupskaya was born into a reasonably well-to-do family in 1869. Her father had been an officer in the **czar's** army before she was born, but had been dismissed for being too gentle with Polish protesters, and thereafter had a series of different jobs. Her mother wrote children's books. Nadezhda was well educated and, like her future husband, slowly became convinced of the correctness of Marx's revolutionary teachings. She first met Vladimir Ulyanov at a marxist discussion group in 1894.

▶ *This photo of Lenin's wife, Nadezhda Krupskaya, was taken around the time the two met in St. Petersburg.*

A revolutionary network

In March 1895, the authorities finally gave Vladimir permission to travel abroad. His trip lasted for several months. He took the opportunity to get medical advice on his stomach troubles, but his main goal was to visit the leaders of Russian **marxism,** all of whom were living in exile in western Europe. In Geneva, Switzerland, he met the most important of these leaders—Georgi Plekhanov—and the two men got along well. Plekhanov was pleased to hear that he had so many followers back in Russia, and they discussed Vladimir's idea of launching a newspaper. After meeting several other prominent marxists, Vladimir returned to **St. Petersburg** full of optimism.

With the help of a new **ally,** Yuli Martov, Vladimir shifted the emphasis of their political activity in St. Petersburg from discussion about theories to agitation among the workers. He wrote a leaflet for striking textile workers explaining their legal rights. He had now

▲ *Lenin (center) and Yuli Martov (seated at right) are shown here with a group of fellow marxists in St. Petersburg in 1895.*

done something to really worry the authorities, so he was arrested on December 9, 1895.

Vladimir spent the next fourteen months in the St. Petersburg prison awaiting his sentence and working on his future book, *The Development of Capitalism in Russia.* His family sent in food and pencils, and he smuggled out invisible messages written in milk—heating the messages turned the writing brown.

Dancing feet

"Vladimir Ilyich said that in the preliminary prison he always polished the cell floor himself since this was a good form of gymnastics. And so he acted like a real old floor-polisher—with his hands held behind him, he would begin to dance to and fro across the cell with a brush or a rag under his foot."

(Dmitri Ulyanov, remembering a conversation with his older brother)

Siberia

In January 1897, Vladimir was finally sentenced to three years' exile in Siberia. This proved easier than he might have expected. He was sent to Shushenskoye in "Siberian Italy," so-called because of its mild climate. Nadezhda Krupskaya was sentenced in 1898. She was allowed to join him on the condition that they married, and they did so in 1898. Vladimir worked hard on his book and enjoyed himself in the Siberian wilderness, hunting, fishing, and gathering wild mushrooms.

▲ This cottage, in Shushenskoye, Siberia, is where Vladimir and his wife, Nadezhda Krupskaya, spent their years of exile.

In the summer of 1898 he finished *The Development of Capitalism in Russia*. His main argument, supported by a large number of statistics, was that Russia was becoming a **capitalist** country just like those in western Europe. This implied that Russia should also have a middle-class **democracy,** and that this would lead to a **socialist** revolution. As the century drew to an end, Vladimir was laying the plans for his future actions.

5 | A Party to Lead

When his term of Siberian exile came to an end in 1900, Vladimir was again granted permission to leave Russia. First, however, he traveled back to **St. Petersburg.** He was full of ideas and enthusiasm for the struggle ahead, but also worried by what he had heard of all the arguments among the Russian **marxist** exiles. On arrival, he found that there was indeed little or no agreement on what should be done next. The Russian Social-Democratic Workers' Party had been formed in 1898 and was led by Georgi Plekhanov, but there was little agreement as to what the party should do. Some wanted to let **trade unions**

▲ Vladimir is shown here in 1900, soon after his release from exile.

make all the important decisions. Others wanted to launch a new terrorist campaign. Some seemed quite happy to wait until the middle classes had overthrown the **czar** and created a democracy before they began seriously working for **socialism.**

Iskra

Vladimir's first priority was the creation of a newspaper. This, he thought, would provide a link between the exiles and their fellow marxists inside Russia, and would also help to create a unified **party policy.** Plekhanov agreed with him, and the first edition of *Iskra*—which means "The Spark"—was printed in the last few days of 1900.

◀ *Georgi Plekhanov, at left, was the father of Russian marxism. He was a founding member of the Russian Social-Democratic Workers' Party and an editor of* Iskra.

Vladimir was only one of six editors—all of whom also wrote—but he was the most active and the most determined.

The first *Iskra* editorial was a clear message to all those **marxists** who were happy to wait for either the middle class or the working class to suddenly produce a revolution in Russia. The whole point of a **Socialist** party, he wrote, was to urge the masses on, to point out where their real interests lay when they did not realize it for themselves. The party's job was to lead, not follow.

The need for organization

"If we have a strongly organized party, a single strike may grow into a political demonstration, into a political victory over the **regime.** If we have a strongly organized party, a rebellion in a single locality may spread into a victorious revolution."

(Vladimir Ulyanov, writing in the first edition of *Iskra*, December 1900)

What Is to Be Done?

With the paper up and running, Vladimir wrote a very influential pamphlet explaining his ideas. He gave it the same title—*What Is to Be Done?*—as the novel by Chernyshevski that had so influenced him and his older brother. Vladimir's work, however, had a very different theme. He wrote a practical pamphlet, almost a manual, on how to create a revolution in Russia. He signed it with a new pseudonym, or false name: he would now always be known as Lenin.

According to *What Is to Be Done?*, the only real option was to create a party that operated in secret and was disciplined, united, and highly centralized. The party's job was to convince the working class that its arguments were right. The working class would then overthrow the **czarist** government and ease the sufferings of the Russian people.

This made sense to Lenin's supporters. They felt there was no hope of organizing support in full view of the government— the organizers would simply be arrested. It was also clear that a party operating "underground" would need direction from a single-minded central leadership as well as strong discipline.

However, there was opposition to Lenin's views. Some thought that what seemed to be his fondness for direct action verged on support of terrorism, while some were simply jealous of his growing importance in the party. More importantly, some pointed out how **undemocratic** his plans were: **party policy** would be decided by only a very few people.

Home life

During this period Lenin and Krupskaya were living in Munich, Germany. He wrote, she acted as his secretary, and her mother, who also lived with them, did the cooking.

Lenin needed absolute silence in order to work, and was even known to walk around his study on tiptoe to avoid disturbing his own train of thought. For exercise he often went on long bicycle rides.

The couple had not had any children, which was a source of great sadness to them both. In their leisure hours they read novels and frequently attended the theater and concerts. Lenin, like most of the Ulyanovs, was passionately fond of music by the composer Richard Wagner, and sometimes he would get so excited by the music that he had to leave the concert hall. All through his life Lenin would strive to repress his own passionate nature. He was determined to be guided by his mind and not by his feelings.

In 1902 Lenin and Krupskaya moved to London, England, where it had been decided that *Iskra* would be produced. Lenin loved the libraries and parks there, but hated English food. He and Krupskaya often took long rides around the city on double-decker buses with open tops. One morning, a young revolutionary named Leon Trotsky came to the house to introduce himself. He and Lenin quickly became friends.

The Second Congress

The long-awaited Second Congress of the Russian Social-Democratic Workers' Party took place, first in Brussels, Belgium, and then in London in 1903. The differences of opinion inside the party had been buried for awhile, but they had not gone away, and the Congress proved to be a bad-tempered and divisive event. On one important vote, Lenin and his supporters won by a majority, and emphasized this by calling themselves the **Bolsheviks,** or "those of the majority."

Most of the time he found himself outvoted, and it became clear that he had few supporters among the party's members in Russia. More supported the **Mensheviks,** or "those of the minority." In the arguments that followed, he ended up resigning from the committee that ran *Iskra*.

By the start of 1904, Lenin was at a low point. His stomach problems, headaches, and sleeping problems had returned, and many Bolsheviks were now refusing to support him. That summer, he and Krupskaya took a long vacation in the Alps to get away from it all. When they returned, Lenin felt ready to reorganize those supporters he still had, call together a new Party Congress, and start a new newspaper to rival *Iskra*. The Bolsheviks, he was convinced, would win the struggle for power within the party.

▲ *Above are delegates to the Second Congress of the Russian Social-Democratic Workers' Party in 1903. Lenin is second from the left in the top row; his wife, Nadezhda Krupskaya, is at far left in the bottom row.*

6 Waiting in the Wings

On Sunday, January 9, 1905, a peaceful group of people approached the Winter Palace of **Czar** Nicholas II in **St. Petersburg,** armed only with a petition asking for **civil rights** and greater **democracy.** The czar's soldiers opened fire and more than 70 marchers were killed. "Bloody Sunday," as it was called, ushered in more than a year of disturbances throughout the Russian Empire. Strikes and demonstrations became an almost daily affair, and the czar's authority was further weakened by a series of defeats in the Russo-Japanese War. New councils, or **soviets,** sprang up everywhere. Refused democracy by the czar, the people decided to elect their own governments all across the Russian Empire.

▼ *This painting shows the czar's troops attacking the peaceful demonstration on Bloody Sunday (January 9, 1905).*

Watching from a distance

The **marxist** exiles in western Europe were overjoyed by the revolutionary activity in their native land, but argued amongst themselves about how they should react. In April 1905, a Party Congress was called with the intention of unifying the divided party, but most of Lenin's opponents refused to attend. He was therefore able to reassert his authority over his **Bolshevik** colleagues. As usual, he favored direct action. An **armed insurrection** was needed, he told the Congress. A revolutionary government should be set up, the property of the rich taken away, and mass terror unleashed. Lenin sounded like a real revolutionary, and his words electrified the audience.

Call to action

"The phenomenon in which we are interested is the armed struggle . . . . Armed struggle pursues two different aims, which must be strictly distinguished: in the first place, this struggle aims at assassinating individuals, chiefs, and subordinates in the army and police; in the second place, it aims at the confiscation of monetary funds both from government and from private persons. The confiscated funds go partly into the treasury of the party, partly for the special purpose of arming and preparing for an uprising, and partly for the maintenance of persons engaged in the struggle we are describing."

(Lenin, writing about guerrilla warfare in 1906)

As the year passed, however, Lenin made no move to return to Russia. Many of his fellow marxists did so—Trotsky became a leading member of the **St. Petersburg** Soviet. Lenin felt sure that he would be arrested if he returned, however, and did not see how his own arrest would help the revolution. It was only when the czar issued his October Manifesto, promising civil rights for the Russian people and pardoning all political exiles, that Lenin felt able to set foot once more in his homeland.

Back in Russia

Before returning to Russia, Lenin wrote to the **Bolsheviks'** Combat Committee and bitterly complained that "there has been talk about bombs for more than a year and yet not a single bomb has been made!" By early November, however, when he arrived back in **St. Petersburg,** the revolutionary enthusiasm had clearly passed its peak. Lenin set out to understand exactly what had happened, attending meeting after meeting and talking to as many people as he could.

Meanwhile, the **czar's regime** was regaining its strength and confidence, and in the summer of 1906 Lenin and other Bolshevik leaders thought it wise to leave St. Petersburg. They moved to Finland, then a fairly detached portion of the Russian Empire, and for about a year tried to run the party from there. Eventually even Finland proved to be unsafe.

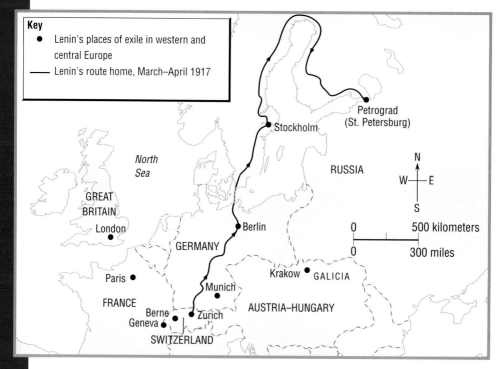

Key
- Lenin's places of exile in western and central Europe
— Lenin's route home, March–April 1917

Petrograd (St. Petersburg)

Stockholm

North Sea

RUSSIA

GREAT BRITAIN

London

Berlin

GERMANY

Paris

Krakow • GALICIA

Munich

FRANCE

AUSTRIA–HUNGARY

Berne • Zurich
Geneva •

SWITZERLAND

N
W — E
S

0 — 500 kilometers
0 — 300 miles

▲ *This map shows Lenin's places of exile from 1901 to 1917.*

Lenin, having been warned that a police raid was going to take place, decided to catch a ferry to Sweden from an island off the Finnish coast. To reach the island he had to walk across a half-frozen bay, and the two local guides who escorted him were both too drunk to offer much help. On one occasion the ice broke beneath him, and Lenin barely managed to scramble to safety.

Exile once more

Despite Lenin's objections, the Bolshevik headquarters was moved to Paris in 1908. For the next four years, he and Krupskaya shared a house there with her mother and his youngest sister, Maria. Maria, like Lenin's older sister Anna and brother Dmitri, was active in the revolutionary movement.

In Paris Lenin read, wrote, and schemed. Each day he rode his bicycle to the famous library, the Bibliothèque Nationale, and on one occasion he was knocked off his bike by a car. He used his legal training to sue the motorist, who, much to Lenin's glee, turned out to be a nobleman.

Lenin's "Hm"

"He enjoyed fun, and when he laughed his whole body shook, really bursting with laughter, sometimes until tears came into his eyes. There was an endless scale of shade and meaning in his inarticulate 'hm'—ranging from bitter sarcasm to cautious doubt, and there was often in it the keen humor given only to one who sees far ahead and knows well the satanic absurdities [the terrible ridiculousness] of life."

(Russian writer Maxim Gorky, who first met Lenin in 1908)

◀ *Lenin, at left, is playing chess with fellow Russian marxist A. A. Bogdanov. Both men were staying with the Russian writer Maxim Gorky on the Italian island of Capri in May 1908.*

It was during this period that Lenin began a love affair with another revolutionary, Inessa Armand. It seems certain that she was in love with him and probable that he was in love with her. After two years or so of the affair, Lenin was forced to choose between Armand and his wife. He chose Krupskaya. His wife was his coworker and nothing, not even love, was more important to Lenin than his work.

War

In 1912, Lenin and Krupskaya moved to the Polish city of Krakow, in what was then **Austria-Hungary.** They had been there for two years when **World War I** suddenly broke out. As Russian nationals in Austria–Hungary they qualified as **enemy aliens,** and Lenin spent several days in jail while his friends tried to convince the Austrian authorities that Lenin liked the **czar** even less than the Austrians did. Eventually he and Krupskaya were allowed to travel to Switzerland, which was neutral and did not support either side in the war.

Once safe, Lenin was able to review what had happened elsewhere in Europe. The German Social Democrats, supposedly **marxists** like himself, had supported the German emperor and his war! In fact, **Socialists** all over Europe were acting as if a person's country was more important than one's social class. Lenin was outraged. The European working class was being betrayed by its socialist leaders, by people who Lenin thought should have known better.

His answer was to call for civil wars to take place in countries all across Europe. Each national working class, he said, should work for the defeat of its own government. He particularly longed for a Russian defeat, because he thought that would probably mean the end of the czar.

At that time, few supported him. Deprived of contact with Russia and ignored by many of his fellow exiles, he felt increasingly alone. The death of his mother, whom he dearly loved, was another blow.

As always he hid from his feelings by working. In 1916, he wrote the pamphlet *Imperialism: A Higher Stage of Capitalism*. It became one of the most influential works of the twentieth century. The whole world economy was now linked together, he wrote. This meant that **capitalism** was now vulnerable everywhere—not only in the rich, developed countries like Great Britain, Germany, and the United States (as Marx had said), but in the poorer, less developed ones like Russia as well.

Lenin wondered when the first revolutions would occur. In January 1917, a **pessimistic** Lenin said in a meeting that "we, the old people, perhaps won't survive until the decisive battles of the forthcoming revolution."

29

7 Two Revolutions

In February 1917, the **czarist regime** finally began to break apart under the strains of **World War I.** Demonstrations multiplied, strikes erupted, and the **soviets** sprang back to life. The czar, realizing that he could no longer rely on his soldiers, was forced to give up his throne. A provisional, or temporary, government was set up. It did not take Russia out of the war.

News of the czar's fall reached the exiles in Switzerland in March. Lenin celebrated for only one day. This was the beginning, not the end. He sent messages to the **Bolsheviks** in Petrograd (**St. Petersburg's** new name), and demanded that there be no cooperation with the **Mensheviks** and no support for the war. In an open letter to the Russian people he told them: "You performed miracles of proletarian [working class] heroism yesterday in overthrowing the czarist **monarchy** . . . . You will again have to perform miracles of heroism to overthrow the rule of the landlords and **capitalists.**"

The April Theses

Lenin had to get back to Russia. The Germans, thinking that the arrival of antiwar campaigners in Petrograd could only benefit them, agreed to let the exiles through. In late March, Lenin, Krupskaya, and 30 others set off on a week-long journey by train and boat through Germany, Sweden, and Finland. They finally arrived at Petrograd's Finland Station on April 3, 1917.

FOR DETAILS ON KEY PEOPLE OF LENIN'S TIME, SEE PAGES 58–59.

Along the way, Lenin had read in a Petrograd paper that Kamenev and Stalin—two Bolshevik leaders—had been offering support to the provisional government. He was furious, and on arrival he wasted no time in making his own position clear. The time had come, he told the crowd outside Finland Station, to destroy capitalism throughout Europe.

The next day he presented a set of plans—his April Theses, as they were called—to the Bolshevik Central Committee. In these he claimed that the temporary government, as a **bourgeois** or middle-class government, could neither end the war nor satisfy the other needs of most of the Russian people. A second, **socialist** revolution was needed. However, the April Theses ignored what had previously been accepted by most **marxists**—that capitalism had to be fully developed in a country before socialism was possible—and they were rejected by thirteen votes to two. One leading Bolshevik called Lenin's April Theses "the delusions of a lunatic."

Winning the argument

Lenin was frustrated, but he did not change his mind. He believed that time was on his side. The temporary government was unable to solve the problems of war and the economy, and sooner or later it would be destroyed by them. The choice then, as Lenin saw it, would be between going backward or forward. By the end of April he had convinced most of the other Bolshevik leaders that he was right.

▼ *Here, Lenin addresses a political meeting in Moscow. The man standing beside the podium (in front) is Leon Trotsky.*

What Russia needed, Lenin said, was an end to the war, **nationalization** of industry and the banks, land for the peasants, workers' control of the factories, and fairer treatment for minorities. Russia needed, he believed, a **Bolshevik** government.

The speaker

"He was neither a great orator nor a first-rate lecturer . . . . He was never boring, on account of his . . . liveliness and the reasoned conviction that drove him. His customary gestures consisted of raising his hand to underline the importance of what he had said, and then bending toward the audience, smiling and earnest, his palms spread out in an act of demonstration: 'It is obvious, isn't it?'"

(Victor Serge, in his *Memoirs of a Revolutionary*)

Leader in waiting

Lenin had started to dress more nicely, having been persuaded to buy a new suit and shoes in Sweden. His trademark floppy worker's cap contrasted with the more formal headgear worn by most political leaders. Unlike most of the leaders, he was obviously enjoying the revolution. He was really in his element.

He was also eating badly and exhausting himself. In late June he decided to take a short break in the country, and as chance would have it this coincided with a major crisis in Petrograd. The temporary government's latest offensive against the Germans was failing badly, and for a few days in mid-July it looked as though popular pressure might bring the government down. The Bolsheviks, including Lenin, waited.

The temporary government took heart, turned on the Bolsheviks, and tried to arrest the party's leaders. Lenin was forced into hiding in a friend's house and eventually escaped to Finland.

Lenin waited and fretted in Finland, wondering if he had missed his chance. During August, he worked on *State and Revolution*, a pamphlet outlining his hopes for the future. A **socialist** revolution would create a leadership of the workers and peasants, he wrote. Once all traces of the **capitalist** past had been removed, this government would become more **democratic.** Eventually, under **communism,** the need for a **state** would disappear altogether.

▲ *This attic in a barn at Razliv near Petrograd is where Lenin lived and worked when he went into hiding in the summer of 1917.*

Seizure of power

The situation in Petrograd continued to get worse. The temporary government seemed to be falling apart, and the **Bolsheviks** now had the most representatives in the important Petrograd and Moscow **soviets.** The time for an armed uprising had arrived, Lenin wrote to the other Bolshevik leaders on September 12. They disagreed, and Lenin decided he had to return to Petrograd to persuade them. He finally arrived at the end of the month, disguised as a minister of the Lutheran church. He had shaved off his beard and wore a wig, which he had difficulty keeping on his head.

▶ *Lenin is pictured here without his familiar beard, during his months on the run from the temporary government in the summer of 1917.*

The leader

"A short, stocky figure, with a big head set down on his shoulders, bald and bulging. Little eyes, a snubbish nose, wide, generous mouth, and heavy chin; clean-shaven now but already beginning to bristle with the well-known beard of his past and future. Dressed in shabby clothes, his trousers much too long for him. Unimpressive, to be the idol of a mob, loved and revered as perhaps few leaders in history have been."

(Lenin at a meeting in October 1917, as described by American writer John Reed in *Ten Days That Shook the World*, his famous account of the revolution)

The crucial meeting of the Bolshevik Central Committee took place on October 10. Lenin—angry, impatient, and emotional—spoke for over an hour, and the debate that followed lasted until dawn. An **armed insurrection** was decided on by ten votes to two.

Two weeks later, on the night of October 24, the insurrection began. Leon Trotsky did most of the organizing, and groups of armed party members, many of them soldiers and sailors, seized key locations in Petrograd: the post and telegraph offices, the railroad terminals, the state bank, and the **czar's** Winter Palace. By the evening of the 25th, the city was in the hands of the Bolsheviks. "Lenin's wide-awake eyes rested on my tired face," Trotsky wrote later. "'You know,' he said hesitantly, 'to pass suddenly from persecution and underground living to a position of power . . . it makes one dizzy.' We looked at one another and smiled."

▲ *This was one of the motorized units of Red Guards in Petrograd during the October Revolution.*

35

8 The First Year

Although their control was far from complete, the **Bolsheviks** now set out to form a government for all of Russia. They called it the Council of People's **Commissars,** which was abbreviated as **Sovnarkom.** The All-Russian Congress of **Soviets** approved Lenin's appointment as chairman of Sovnarkom, and the appointment of other Bolshevik leaders to other government jobs. Trotsky, for example, became the commissar for foreign affairs, and Stalin was appointed commissar for nationalities.

Promises ...

During its first winter in power Sovnarkom introduced a series of astonishingly far-reaching decrees, or laws. First, as promised, Lenin announced that Russia was withdrawing from **World War I.** Second, the Decree on Land took away all land owned by the nobility and the Russian Orthodox Church, and handed it over to the peasants.

Free schooling was promised for all children, and women were now to be considered the equals of men. All titles except "citizen" and "comrade" were abolished; there would be no more princes or dukes. The maximum length of the working day was reduced to eight hours. The minority nations of the Russian Empire, like the Ukraine and Georgia, were to be given more control over their own affairs. These measures, and not the seizure of power, made up the real revolution.

... And threats

Many people, worn down by the chaos of war and tired of dishonest and ineffective rulers, welcomed these changes. However, there were negative reactions as well.

If the changes were to last, the Bolsheviks had to stay in power. This meant taking steps that were much less popular. Newspapers were shut down for encouraging resistance to Sovnarkom. Previously planned elections for a new Constituent Assembly were allowed to go ahead, but the assembly itself was closed down by force by the Bolsheviks because they (the Bolsheviks) won only one quarter of the seats. More importantly, in December 1917 Lenin promoted the creation of the Extraordinary Commission for Combating Counter-Revolution and Sabotage, or **Cheka.** The function of this armed political police force was to defend the revolution against its growing number of enemies within the country.

The need for terror

"The workers and soldiers of Petrograd must realize that no one will help them except themselves. Malpractices [wrongdoings] are blatant, profiteering [making excessive profits] is monstrous, but what have the masses of soldiers and peasants done to combat this? Unless the masses are roused to spontaneous action, we won't get anywhere . . . . Until we apply terror—shooting on the spot—we won't get anywhere. Looters should likewise be dealt with resolutely—by shooting on the spot."

(Lenin, speaking to the leaders of the Petrograd Soviet in January 1918)

Enemies everywhere

The most immediate threat to the Bolsheviks' survival in the winter of 1917 to 1918 was the German Army. The Russians had stopped fighting the Germans, but the German Army was threatening to keep marching eastward if the Bolsheviks did not sign a peace treaty that handed over huge areas of Russia's old empire to Germany. Most of the Bolshevik leaders thought it would be a betrayal of the German working class to sign a deal with their government.

Bolshevik leaders preferred to let the Germans come and then influence them from within. Lenin did not agree. He wanted to sign the treaty because otherwise, he feared, the whole revolution would be swept aside. The argument went on for weeks, until Lenin's threat of resignation finally won him a majority of votes. The Treaty of Brest-Litovsk, ending the war with Germany, was signed on March 3, 1918.

▲ Lenin reads Pravda, *the newspaper of the* **Communist** *Party of the Soviet Union, at his desk in the* **Kremlin** *on October 16, 1918. Pravda is the Russian word for "truth."*

There was no shortage of other enemies for the Bolsheviks to face. The other revolutionary groups—the **Mensheviks,** the **Socialist** Revolutionaries (the party that represented most peasants), and the **anarchists** (who wanted to abolish all types of government)—all complained and plotted, but for the moment they were the least of Lenin's worries.

Many peasants, dissatisfied with the price they were being paid for grain, refused to sell it at all. The shortages of food in the cities grew more serious. The upper classes—who had lost property and power in the revolution—had not given up hope of getting it back, and **White Armies** led by officers of the old Imperial Army sprang into existence in several areas. The **czar's allies** in **World War I,** who felt betrayed by the Bolsheviks' peace treaty with Germany and were alarmed at the threat of a spreading revolution, sent troops to help the White Armies.

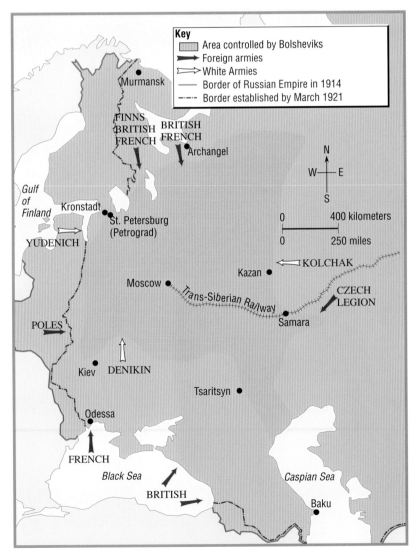

Key

- ▨ Area controlled by Bolsheviks
- ➤ Foreign armies
- ▷ White Armies
- — Border of Russian Empire in 1914
- –·–· Border established by March 1921

▲ *This map shows Russia during the civil war, from 1918 to 1920.*

▲ *This armored train of the Tenth Red Army is pictured in the town of Tsaritsyn. It is leaving for the front during the first year of the civil war.*

At the helm

While the new **Red Army** of revolutionary fighters, under Trotsky's direction, tried to counter these threats, Lenin worked away in the new Russian capital of Moscow. He and Krupskaya had an apartment in the **Kremlin,** but she too had a full-time job—as a deputy **commissar** for education—and they did not see much of each other.

Lenin was not safe even in Moscow. One time, his car was fired on by his own trigger-happy guards; another time, criminals held him up at gunpoint. In August 1918 he was shot and seriously wounded by Fanya Kaplan, a **socialist** revolutionary. The **Cheka's** response was savage: Kaplan and hundreds of others were shot.

By this time Lenin's **regime** was clearly fighting for its life, and terror was one way of fighting back. If Lenin had any regrets about how bloodstained his regime was becoming, he kept them to himself.

An enemy's impression

"He looked at the first glance more like a provincial grocer than a leader of men. Yet in those steely eyes there was something that arrested my attention, something in that quizzing, half-contemptuous, half-smiling look which spoke of boundless self-confidence and conscious superiority."

(British diplomat R.H. Bruce Lockhart, who talked to Lenin early in 1918 about possible cooperation between their two governments)

Most likely he had none. He simply told himself that the revolution's survival was more important than middle-class morality. When the news of the **czar's** execution reached him during a meeting in July 1918, he simply passed on the message to those around the table and then continued with what he had been saying.

▲ *Here, Lenin speaks in Red Square on the first anniversary of the October Revolution: October 26, 1918.*

Key dates: 1917–1918

1917	• February	First Russian Revolution
	• April	Lenin returns to Russia; writes April Theses
	• July	Lenin forced into hiding
	• October	Second Russian Revolution brings **Bolsheviks** to power
	• December	Formation of Cheka
1918	• March	The Treaty of Brest-Litovsk ends war with Germany
	• July	Execution of czar and family

9 Fighting for Survival

In November 1918, **World War I** ended in a German defeat. Lenin cancelled the Treaty of Brest-Litovsk and forced the Germans out of the areas they had once occupied. There were still other foreign troops on Russian soil, including the British in the province of Archangel, the French in the Crimea, and the Americans and Japanese in eastern Siberia. The **Bolsheviks,** who in March 1918 had renamed themselves the **Communist** Party, decided to form the Communist International, or **Comintern,** to fight against **capitalist** governments everywhere. **Marxists** from all over the world were invited to attend the first Congress in March 1919.

▲ *Lenin (second from right) chairs a meeting at the first Congress of Comintern in the Kremlin, in March 1919.*

Welcome to the revolution

"'Have you brought your families with you? I could put them up in palaces, which I know is very nice on some occasions, but it is impossible to heat them. You'd better go to Moscow. Here, we are besieged people in a besieged city. Hunger riots may start, the Finns may swoop on us, the British may attack. Typhus has killed so many people that we can't manage to bury them; luckily they are frozen. If work is what you want, there's plenty of it!' And she told passionately of the Soviet achievement: school building, children's centers, relief for pensioners, free medical assistance, the theaters open to all . . ."

(Victor Serge, recounting his group's welcome to Petrograd
by Bolshevik leader Lilina Zinoviev in January 1919)

Some of the foreign troops were withdrawn in the first half of 1919. By that time, however, the homegrown **White Armies** in Siberia, the Ukraine, and northwestern Russia were mounting a serious threat to Lenin's government.

In the Kremlin

After recovering from being shot Lenin returned to his office in the **Kremlin.** He worked as hard as ever and expected the same from others. He demanded punctuality and sometimes fined latecomers. He forbade smoking in his presence. Despite all this, coworkers usually found him to be considerate, and strangers meeting him for the first time were usually impressed. The British writer H. G. Wells thought that "this amazing little man, with his frank admission of the immensity and complication of the project of communism . . . was very refreshing."

◀ *Here, Lenin talks to the British writer H. G. Wells in his **Kremlin** office.*

Lenin expected no special privileges and took none. His wages were little more than an ordinary worker's; he ate the same food as his staff and lined up to have his hair cut like everyone else. In the winter his apartment was no better heated than any other.

Winning the war

The worst year of the civil war was 1919, but by its end the **White Armies** had been repelled. Although the peasants (who still formed the vast majority of the population) had no great love for the **communists,** they liked the White Armies less. At least the communists had given them their land.

In 1920, the last White Armies were defeated and a Polish invasion of the Ukraine was pushed back by the **Red Army** almost to the gates of Warsaw, the Polish capital. Lenin hoped the Red Army might carry revolution to the whole of Europe, but the Poles fought back and by the end of the year the armies were roughly back where they had started. After three years of terrible and destructive conflict, Russia was once more at peace.

Counting the cost

The cost of the civil war was enormous. The economy was in ruins, with both industrial and agricultural production a fraction of what they had been before the revolution. The value of money had sunk and almost everything, including food, was in short supply. Life remained harsh and difficult for most Russians.

Politically, things looked better for the Communist Party. They had won the war and were in undisputed charge of the country. Victory, however, had been achieved at a terrible cost. In order to win the war, Lenin and the senior party members, the **Politburo**, had been forced to make more and more decisions without involving the **soviets.** Power had shifted to the politburo, and **democracy** in the party was virtually dead.

Feeling the strain

Lenin was not the man he had been in 1917. He still suffered from lack of sleep, headaches, and stomach problems. Although only in his early fifties, he was now experiencing minor heart attacks as well. Toward the end of 1920 the death of his old love Inessa Armand, still a political colleague, hit him hard. Some friends thought he was never the same again.

Lenin knew that the communist revolution was nowhere near complete. It had survived the war, but if it were to survive in times of peace then extreme measures would need to be taken. But which should he take? Without the help of other revolutions in Europe there seemed no hope of a great leap forward. So perhaps, even at the moment of victory, it was time for a cautious step backward.

◀ Lenin, facing the camera, is shown here with Leon Trotsky, the chief organizer of the October Revolution and founder of the Red Army. After Lenin's death, Trotsky was slowly eased from power and sent into exile by Stalin and his **allies.**

10 Second Thoughts?

Before Lenin could introduce the measures he thought necessary, one last huge revolt shook his government. In March 1921, the sailors at the Kronstadt Naval Base near Petrograd, who had been among the most enthusiastic supporters of the revolution, rose up in rebellion, demanding a restoration of **democracy** and the powers of the **soviets.** They wanted, they said, a free **socialist** democracy.

Lenin and his colleagues were not prepared to listen or negotiate. They thought the sailors were being dangerously unrealistic. Such a policy, they thought, would risk the loss of everything that three long years of war had secured. They ordered **Red Army** units across the frozen Gulf of Finland to crush the rebellion. Thousands were killed or imprisoned.

▲ *Soldiers of the Red Army advance across the frozen Gulf of Finland to attack the rebel-held naval fortress of Kronstadt in March 1921.*

Disillusionment

"One by one the embers of our hopes have died out. Terror and despotism [tyranny] have crushed the life born in October . . . . The Revolution is dead; its spirit cries in the wilderness."

(American **anarchist** Alexander Berkman writing in his diary about the Kronstadt rebellion)

The NEP

While the Kronstadt Naval Base was being stormed, the **Communist** Party was holding its Tenth Congress. It was here that Lenin formally introduced his **New Economic Policy (NEP).** Its main features were an end to the official taking of grain from the peasants—from now on they were obliged to give a fixed amount to the **state** but could keep or sell the rest—and the return to private ownership of businesses employing twenty workers or less. It was now legal again to trade and make a profit. There were even plans to restore trading with the **capitalist** countries.

This freeing-up of the economy was more popular with the country than it was with many in the party. They thought Lenin was reintroducing capitalism, and this after fighting a long war in the name of communism! He told them it was only a temporary retreat. To counter the dangers of loosening control over the economy, the party planned to strengthen its control over both the country and itself. The use of terror would continue, and groups inside the party were banned. Anyone who refused to support **party policy** would be expelled. The price of economic recovery was even less democracy, even less political freedom.

Illness

Getting the party to accept the **NEP** was hard work. By June, Lenin was so exhausted that the **Politburo** insisted he take a month off to recover in the village of Gorki, 20 miles (30 kilometers) south of Moscow. That month in Gorki turned into three months, and then six. Lenin continued to work and often traveled into Moscow to lead meetings, but he was seriously ill. The doctors brought in to examine him could not agree on what was wrong. Then, on May 25, 1922, he suffered a massive stroke that paralyzed his whole right side and made speaking difficult.

Krupskaya and Lenin's youngest sister, Maria, came to look after him full time. Against most expectations he began to recover. He read books, played with a dog he had adopted, chatted with Stalin—now the party's general secretary and a frequent visitor—and interested himself in a nearby farm. In October 1922, he felt well enough to return to the **Kremlin** and resume some of his duties.

FOR DETAILS ON KEY PEOPLE OF LENIN'S TIME, SEE PAGES 58–59.

▲ This is Lenin in Gorki in August 1922, with two local children, his sister Anna (wearing the hat), and his wife, Nadezhda Krupskaya.

Perhaps he was fooling himself, perhaps not. He was still the most respected figure in the government; people still listened to what he had to say. Fearing that his time was short, he probably wanted to cram as much into it as possible. The future of the revolution he had led was naturally uppermost in his mind. Who should succeed him as leader and what should the policies be?

Testament

Lenin had no clear-cut favorite to succeed him, as he made clear in the letter to the Party Congress which is generally known as his "Testament." Leon Trotsky, Grigori Zinoviev, Lev Kamenev, and Nikolai Bukharin all had their strengths and weaknesses, according to Lenin. But he was very clear about whom he did not want. Lenin had become caught up in several disputes with Stalin over the previous year and had also discovered that Stalin had been very rude to Krupskaya over the telephone. Stalin, he advised the others, should be removed from his post.

Last words

"Having become general secretary, Comrade Stalin has concentrated unlimited power in his hands, and I am not sure that he will always use that power with sufficient care . . . . Stalin is too rude and this failing, which is entirely acceptable in relations among us **communists,** is not acceptable in a general secretary. I therefore suggest that the comrades find a means of moving Stalin from this post and giving the job to someone else who is superior to Comrade Stalin in every way, that is, more patient, more loyal, more respectful, and more considerate to his comrades . . ."

(Excerpts from Lenin's "Testament," written in December 1922 and January 1923)

49

When it came to policies, Lenin's advice was less clear. He continued to believe in the necessity of terrorizing opponents of the party, but in all other respects he seemed to be becoming more moderate. In several articles written during these months, he stressed the need to reduce the size of government institutions, to learn from other countries, and to develop the revolution slowly and cautiously.

How far Lenin might have gone down that road, and how much he might have rolled back the overpowering **state** he had done so much to create, will never be known. In March 1923, another stroke paralyzed him and took away his power of speech. This time there was no real recovery, only a half-life that lasted until his death on January 21, 1924. He was only 53 years old.

A newspaper headline

"In a compartment full of fat, stodgy men, someone opened a newspaper and I saw: *Death of Lenin*. Then these men talked about the death, showing that they felt something unique and very great had passed. I looked at their faces, folk from another world, Austrian **petty-bourgeois** closed to all new ideas, lamenting the death of a revolutionary . . ."

(Russian revolutionary Victor Serge, riding on a
European train in late January 1924)

An incomplete farewell

The funeral took place six days later. Across the Soviet Union trains stopped, boats moored, and factory whistles blew. In Red Square, in the heart of Moscow, the crowd sang the **communist** anthem the "Internationale," and Lenin's body was lowered into a vault in front of the **Kremlin** wall. The corpse did not stay there for long, however. The **Politburo,** allegedly at Stalin's suggestion, decided to embalm the body and lay it in a **mausoleum.** Even in death Lenin was expected to offer leadership and inspiration—to be, in effect, an immortal leader. Krupskaya protested, but to no avail. Her wishes, like her husband's "Testament," were ignored.

▲ Above, Moscow's Red Square is pictured during Lenin's funeral in 1924. The banner on the right reads, "Lenin's grave is the cradle of liberty of humankind."

11 Legacy

Many people believe that the Second Russian Revolution of 1917, the October Revolution, was one of the most important political events of the twentieth century. Vladimir Ilyich Lenin was more responsible for bringing that revolution about than anyone else. It was he who insisted on starting the newspaper that inspired many Russian revolutionaries, and he who argued loudest for the sort of disciplined party that could successfully mount a revolution. From the end of his Siberian exile in 1900 to his seizure of power in 1917, he pushed his party to the limit, urging it to go where most members feared to tread. It was he who provided the theory, the political justification, for each daring step forward in forcefully argued pamphlets and books. Revolutions are not made by one man, but it is hard to imagine the **Bolshevik** Revolution without Lenin.

Once power had been seized, he seemed to know exactly what was required to keep it. In 1918 and 1921, Bolshevik control was close to evaporating. On each occasion, under great opposition, Lenin managed to push through the right measures—the Treaty of Brest-Litovsk in 1918 and the **New Economic Policy (NEP)** in 1921—to save the day for his party. Without Lenin it is hard to believe that the Soviet Union would have lasted more than a few years.

Wider influence

Lenin's influence outside the Soviet Union was immense and continues to be meaningful. The changes announced and introduced by his government—like the dramatic reduction of wealth and privilege, equality for women and minority nationalities, and free education and health care—inspired people everywhere with the promise of a better, fairer society.

Although putting these plans into practice in the Soviet Union often proved ineffective, too costly in human suffering, or both, the fact that the country stood for such ideals was important in itself. After the Bolshevik Revolution, the **Western** colonial powers could never feel quite so secure again, and Lenin's political methods influenced many young revolutionaries in poorer parts of the world, inspiring the growth of secretive, highly organized parties dedicated to the overthrow of colonial rule. For much of its existence, the Soviet Union acted as a deterrent to **capitalism** in the poorer parts of the world and as a source of support for governments at odds with the great powers of the West.

A difficult call

Inside the Soviet Union the dream of **socialism** had turned sour within ten years of Lenin's death. By 1929, Stalin had abandoned the NEP in favor of **crash industrialization** and the **collectivization of agriculture,** both of which eventually brought levels of terror and intimidation—some estimates claim twenty million deaths—undreamed of in Lenin's day. How responsible was Lenin for the mistakes and evils of his successors? Was the Soviet Union he left behind **inevitably** doomed to this sort of fate?

▶ *Five days after Lenin's death, Stalin, at right, promised the* **Communist** *Party of the U.S.S.R. that he would continue Lenin's work.*

These are difficult questions to answer. There are two clear arguments in Lenin's favor. First, he did try to get rid of Stalin, and could hardly be held responsible for the other **Bolshevik** leaders' failure to take notice of his "Testament." Secondly, he argued for a slow pace of development and a lessening of **state** control in the last months of his active political life. He had an all too brief period in which to address the problems that faced Russia at the end of the civil war, before the onset of his illness. If Lenin had lived longer, some say that the Soviet Union might have revealed a more human face to the rest of the world.

There are two strong arguments against this. First, it was Lenin who founded the **Cheka** and encouraged its use of terror as a political weapon. Perhaps the **regime** during the civil war needed these harsh methods to survive, but the **NEP** was then used after the war to justify more of the same. Lenin found it all too easy to ignore his own morals when he felt other people had to suffer for the good of the revolution. He does not seem to have asked himself whether a revolution that needed to defend itself in this way for the foreseeable future was worth having.

A call to arms

"An oppressed class that does not strive to learn to use arms, to acquire arms, only deserves to be treated like slaves. We cannot, unless we have become **bourgeois** pacifists or opportunists, forget that we are living in a class society from which there is no way out, nor can there be, save through the class struggle."

(Lenin writing in 1917, explaining what he sees as the necessity of class struggle)

Second, Lenin closed down **democracy** in the country at large, and then inside his own party as well. He always had good arguments for this, but the suspicion remains that the only person he trusted to be in charge was himself. Lenin always thought he knew best, and he distrusted the motives of anyone who disagreed with him. He was **undemocratic** by nature.

An inspiration and a warning

In the Soviet Union, Lenin remained a national hero right up until the fall of **communism** in 1991. His face stared down from schoolroom walls and his statues stood in city squares. Each day thousands of Soviet citizens and foreign tourists visited his embalmed body in its Red Square **mausoleum.**

Now that Russia and the rest of the former Soviet Union have abandoned communism, Lenin has become less of a living symbol and more of a historical figure. The ideals that inspired the Bolshevik Revolution—and which in the end were so completely betrayed by it—are still alive in the world today. Lenin, who played a huge part in making that revolution, now serves as both an inspiration and a warning to those who seek to follow in his footsteps.

▼ *The people in this line are visitors waiting to view Lenin's mausoleum.*

Timeline

1870	Vladimir Ilyich Ulyanov (later called Lenin) is born on April 10 in Simbirsk.
1879	Vladimir begins schooling at the Simbirsk Gimnazia.
1886	His father dies.
1887	His older brother Alexander is executed for planning to assassinate the **czar.**
	Vladimir finishes his schooling and enrolls at Kazan University.
	In December he is expelled for taking part in student protests.
1890–91	Ulyanov earns a law degree as an **external student** at **St. Petersburg** University, and works as a lawyer in Samara.
1893	He moves to St. Petersburg.
1895	Ulyanov visits leading Russian **marxists** in western and central Europe.
	He is arrested in St. Petersburg for illegal political activities.
1895–97	Ulyanov is imprisoned in St. Petersburg.
1897	He is exiled to Siberia.
1898	He marries Nadezhda Krupskaya.
	The Russian Social-Democratic Workers' Party is formed.
1900	Lenin is released from Siberian exile.
	He travels to western Europe.
	Iskra is published.
1901	Lenin writes *What Is to Be Done?*
1903	The Russian Social-Democratic Workers' Party splits into **Bolshevik** and **Menshevik** factions.
1905	This is a year of political turmoil in Russia.
	Lenin returns to Russia in November.
1906	Lenin moves to Finland to avoid arrest.
1907	He returns to western Europe.
1908–12	Lenin lives in Paris.
1912–14	He lives in Galicia, a Polish area of the **Austro-Hungarian** Empire.

1914	**World War I** begins.
1914–17	Lenin lives in Switzerland. He writes *Imperialism: The Highest Stage of Capitalism*.
1917	In February, the First Russian Revolution occurs. In April, Lenin arrives back in Russia and writes his *April Theses*.
	In July, he is forced into hiding.
	In October, the Second Russian Revolution brings the Bolsheviks to power.
	The czar decrees an end to the war and gives land to the peasants.
	The **Cheka** is established.
1918	The Constituent Assembly is closed.
	The Treaty of Brest-Litovsk is signed.
	The czar and his family are executed.
1918–20	A civil war is fought in Russia.
1921	The Kronstadt Rebellion takes place.
	The **New Economic Policy (NEP)** is introduced.
	Lenin's health deteriorates.
1922	He suffers a massive stroke in May.
1922–23	From December to February, he writes a letter to congress (his "Testament"), which is critical of Stalin, and several articles recommending a moderation of the revolution.
	He suffers another massive stroke in March 1923.
1924	Lenin dies on January 21 at the age of 53. His body is embalmed and placed in a **mausoleum** in Red Square.
1929	After several years of fighting between Russian groups, Stalin emerges as the single leader of the Soviet Union and enforces a third revolution, featuring a **crash industrialization** program, overall **state** planning, and the **collectivization of agriculture.**
1989–91	**Communism** collapses and the Soviet Union breaks up into fifteen separate countries.

Key People of Lenin's Time

Bukharin, Nikolai Ivanovich (1888–1938). Born in Moscow, Bukharin became politically active as a student during the 1905 revolution. He lived as a revolutionary inside Russia until 1912, when he was arrested and exiled. He escaped to western Europe and returned to Russia in 1917. While there was a chance of further revolutions in Europe he argued for the **Bolsheviks** to make trouble wherever they could, but when it became clear that these revolutions would not take place he joined Lenin in arguing for a slow and peaceful progress towards **socialism** in Russia. He was executed by Stalin in 1938.

Gorky, Maxim (1868–1936). This Russian writer was also involved in revolutionary politics. He was briefly imprisoned in 1905, and then lived in western European exile until 1917. He became both a supporter of the Bolshevik Revolution and an important critic of its excesses.

Kamenev, Lev Borisovich (1883–1936). Borisovich started his revolutionary activities in 1901 and was a leading Bolshevik during the time leading up to the seizure of power in 1917, which, along with Zinoviev, he initially opposed. After the revolution he was in charge of the Moscow **Communist** Party organization. He was executed by Stalin in 1936.

Martov, Yuli Osipovich (1873–1923). Martov was a Russian **marxist** and one of Lenin's closest colleagues in his earlier days. They fell out in 1903, and Martov became one of the leading **Mensheviks.** He fought the Bolsheviks after 1917, chose to go into exile in 1921, and died in Berlin in 1923.

Marx, Karl (1818–83). Marx was a German philosopher, economist, and political scientist whose theories of social development helped to inspire both socialism and communism (see box on page 13).

Plekhanov, Georgi Valentinovich (1857–1918). Seen as the founder of Russian marxism, Valentinovich founded the Emancipation of Labor Group in 1883 and helped to found the Russian Social-Democratic Workers' Party in 1898. He fell out with Lenin in 1903 on political and personal grounds, and joined the Mensheviks. He was not an active figure in the revolutions of 1917.

Stalin, Joseph Vissarionovich (1878–1953). Stalin was born Joseph Djugashvili in Georgia, by the Black Sea. He was an active member of the Russian Social-Democratic Workers' Party starting around 1900, and a Bolshevik starting in 1903. Stalin endured many periods of Siberian exile between then and the revolution. In 1917, he was appointed **commissar** for nationalities, and in 1922 he was appointed to the powerful position of general secretary of the Communist Party. He survived the criticism included in Lenin's "Testament," out-maneuvered his opponents in the party, and established a one-man **dictatorship** over the Soviet Union. He introduced the programs of **crash industrialization** and the **collectivization of agriculture,** and instituted a reign of terror over the Soviet population that saw many millions either killed or sent to prison camps.

Trotsky, Leon (1879–1940). Trotsky was born Lev Davidovich Bronstein in Yanovka, Ukraine. In 1898, as a young revolutionary, he was arrested and exiled to Siberia. He escaped to western Europe in 1902, but returned to play a starring role as leader of the **St. Petersburg Soviet** of Workers' Deputies in the 1905 Russian Revolution. A great speaker and writer, he worked as a journalist in the **West** until 1917, when he returned again to Russia. He joined the Bolsheviks, supported Lenin when he argued for a Bolshevik revolution, and played a major role in organizing the seizure of power. As Lenin's commissar of war, he created the **Red Army** and led it to victory in the Russian Civil War. After Lenin's death, jealous colleagues and the single-minded Stalin eased him from power. In 1940, he was murdered in Mexico by one of Stalin's secret agents.

Ulyanov, Alexander Ilyich (1866–87). Alexander, Lenin's older brother, was executed by the **regime** of **Czar** Alexander III for his part in planning an attempt on the Czar's life.

Zinoviev, Grigori (1883–1936) Zinoviev became a revolutionary around 1900, and was a leading Bolshevik during the time leading up to the seizure of power in 1917. After the revolution he was in charge of the Petrograd (later Leningrad) party organization. He was head of the **Comintern** from 1919 to 1926. He was executed by Stalin in 1936.

Sources for Further Research

Downing, David. *Joseph Stalin.* Chicago: Heinemann Library, 2001.

Edwards, Judith. *Lenin & the Russian Revolution in World History.* Berkeley Heights, N.J.: Enslow Publishers, 2001.

Gilbert, Adrian. *The Russian Revolution.* New York: Raintree Steck-Vaughn, 1996.

Ritchie, Nigel. *Communism.* New York: Raintree Steck-Vaughn, 2001.

Sherrow, Victoria. *Life During the Russian Revolution.* Farmington Hills, Mich.: Gale Group, 1997.

Taylor, David. *Key Battles of World War I.* Chicago: Heinemann Library, 2001.

Wade, Rex A. *The Bolshevik Revolution & Russian Civil War.* Westport, Conn.: Greenwood Publishing Group, Inc., 2000.

Willoughby, Susan. *The Russian Revolution.* Chicago: Heinemann Library, 1998.

Glossary

allies people or countries that believe in and fight for the same things

anarchist person who rebels against an accepted authority

armed insurrection violent uprising against the government

Austria-Hungary name of the Austrian Empire—made up of present-day Austria and Hungary—from 1867 to 1918

Bolshevik one of two political parties that came out of the 1903 split in the Russian Social-Democratic Workers' Party. *Bolshevik* is Russian for "those of the majority."

bourgeoisie middle-class capitalist class—those who own the industries and banks. The adjective form is "bourgeois."

capitalism economic system in which the production and distribution of goods depend on the wealth of individuals, not governments

Cheka Extraordinary Commission for Combating Counter-Revolution and Sabotage: the police force created by Lenin in December 1917. After World War II it was called the KGB.

civil rights legal rights of all people to the same equal opportunities and benefits

collectivization of agriculture creation of large, jointly owned farms by putting together smaller farms that were once privately owned

Comintern Communist International, an organization formed by the world's communist parties with the aim of promoting world revolution

commissar position of authority in Sovnarkom (the Bolshevik government after October 1917) with particular responsibility for one area of government.

communism in theory, an economic system in which people jointly own all goods, and in which they take goods as they need them. The name was adopted by the Bolsheviks and became associated with the economics and politics developed in the Soviet Union in the mid-twentieth century under Lenin, Stalin, and their successors.

crash industrialization program introduced by Stalin that changed the focus of the Soviet economy from agriculture to industry in a very short period of time

czar (sometimes written "tsar") hereditary ruler of the Russian Empire, similar to a king or emperor

democracy political system in which governments are regularly elected by the majority of the people, or a country in which this system exists

dictatorship government ruled absolutely by an individual called a dictator, in which the majority of the people have no say in how they are governed

enemy alien foreign-born resident who, because of where he or she was born, is considered to be an enemy of the government of the host country

external student person who studies from home rather than at a college or university

inevitable unable to be stopped

Kremlin walled fortress in Moscow that has been the traditional home of Russian leaders almost continuously since the twelfth century

marxism ideas of Karl Marx, especially having to do with equality among all people; a person who believes and acts according to these ideas is called a marxist

mausoleum large tomb or resting place for the dead

Menshevik one of two political parties that came out of the 1903 split in the Russian Social-Democratic Workers' Party. *Menshevik* is Russian for "those of the minority."

monarchy government in which a country or territory is ruled absolutely by a ruler who is usually hereditary

nationalization process by which a government takes the control of businesses and institutions away from private owners

New Economic Policy (NEP) reintroduction of limited and private trading that followed the Russian Civil War

party policy agreed-upon way of thinking and course of action for a political party

pessimistic way of thinking that emphasizes the negative over the positive

petty-bourgeois lower middle class

Politburo Soviet government cabinet; can also mean a small, ruling committee

Red Army army originally formed by the Bolsheviks to defend their revolution in the Russian Civil War. After the civil war it became the official army of the Soviet Union.

regime government currently in power; a form of government

socialism way of organizing society that puts the needs of the community above the short-term wants or needs of the individual; a person who supports this is called a socialist

soviet Russian for "council"

Sovnarkom abbreviation of the Russian name for the Council of People's Commissars, the Bolshevik government formed in 1917

St. Petersburg city on the Gulf of Finland and one-time capital of the Russian Empire. Renamed Petrograd in 1914 and Leningrad in 1924, its name reverted to St. Petersburg once more in 1991.

state politically organized group of people who rule themselves, and who usually occupy their own, separate territory; or, the government made from this group

trade union organization formed to protect the rights of workers

undemocratic not taking into account the wishes of the people

West (usually capitalized) noncommunist countries of Europe and America

White Armies armies fighting against the "red" Bolsheviks in the Russian Civil War. Most people in these armies came from Russia's former ruling class. Some White Armies wanted to bring back the czar; others wanted to restore the government that existed between the two revolutions in 1917.

women's rights the rights of women to legal and social equality with men

World War I international war that involved most of the European nations, as well as Russia, the United States, and countries of the Middle East, from 1914 to 1918

Index